IMAGES
of America

FRANKFORD

IMAGES
of America

FRANKFORD

Brian H. Harris
for the Historical Society of Frankford

ARCADIA
PUBLISHING

Published by Arcadia Publishing
Charleston, South Carolina

Library of Congress Catalog Card Number: 2005920023

For all general information contact Arcadia Publishing at:
Telephone 843-853-2070
Fax 843-853-0044
E-mail sales@arcadiapublishing.com
For customer service and orders:
Toll-Free 1-888-313-2665

Visit us on the Internet at www.arcadiapublishing.com

CONTENTS

Introduction   6

1. Street Scenes   9

2. Churches   29

3. Frankford Hospital   37

4. Schools   43

5. Frankford El and Septa   55

6. Houses   63

7. Sports   77

8. The People of Frankford   89

9. Businesses   99

10. An Ending Walk through Frankford's Past   111

Acknowledgments   128

INTRODUCTION

The book that you are reading is about the Frankford section of Philadelphia, located at the foot of what is known as the northeast section of Philadelphia. It is bordered by the Frankford Creek, Castor Avenue, which forms the western boundary, and the meeting point of Cheltenham and Delaware Avenues to the east.

The history of Frankford can be traced back well over 340 years to the year 1660, when the first European settlers set foot in the area. Before these settlers, the land was inhabited by the Lenni-Lenape tribe of Native Americans. The first European settlers were the Swedes, who operated a gristmill along Frankford Creek and stayed there until 1850.

The Swedes recorded very little of their time in Frankford. We do know that the Quakers soon established themselves and named the area Oxford Township, possibly after Oxford, England, where Sarah Seary's husband, Thomas, was from. Sarah was a Quaker, and meetings were frequently held in her home. Her house is thought to have stood on Bristol Pike, just above Frankford, north of the present Cedar Hill Cemetery. Meetings were held at this place until a log meetinghouse was built by what is now Unity and Waln Streets in Frankford.

Through the 18th century, Frankford thrived as one of the most well-recognized towns in Pennsylvania. Many people stopped at the popular Jolly Post Inn and Tavern, which hosted many events and significant individuals during the Revolutionary War. Five days after the battles of Lexington and Concord, a rider stopped at the Jolly Post to exchange his tired horse. He described the battles to many of the residents of Frankford during his stop. These residents heard of the news before even those in Philadelphia. Marquis de Lafayette was a popular visitor to Frankford and the Jolly Post. Other popular inns were the Cross Keys Hotel, the General Pike Hotel, the Seven Stars Hotel, and the Park Hotel, where the first volunteer fire company organized and the first building association in the United States was founded.

Along with these popular inns, many well-known mansions stood in Frankford. Chalkley Hall was the home of Thomas Chalkley, one of the greatest travelers of his time. Old Port Royal Mansion was located between the present Tacony Street and Frankford Creek and built by Edward Stiles, great-grandson of one of the first settlers of Bermuda. Another was Millsdale, home of famed naval hero Captain Stephen Decatur.

Frankford took part in every war that America called its citizens to after the Revolutionary War. From the War of 1812 to the Civil War to the Great Wars and beyond, many of Frankford's men and women contributed directly to the war effort and answered their country's call to duty.

Frankford at one time was considered one of the most thriving manufacturing sites in the state of Pennsylvania. With companies such as the Frankford Dyeing, Bleaching, and Finishing Works started by Jeremiah Horrocks, the firm of William and Harvey Rowland (who manufactured springs), the pottery business of Issac English, and many of the other manufacturing businesses found that Frankford and its residents contributed greatly to their successes. The most well-known of all of the manufacturing plants was the United States Arsenal on Frankford Creek between the village of Bridesburg and the borough of Frankford, known to many people today as the Frankford Arsenal.

With the growth of industry in Frankford and the availability of employment, the town's population grew, as did the need for places of worship. Besides the Friends meeting house, which was built in 1684, a number of new churches began to surface in the area. The German Reformed (German Calvinist) Church and the Frankford Presbyterian Church were both built in 1770. The Frankford Baptist Church traces back to 1806 and St. Mark's Protestant Episcopal Church roots back to 1820. The Rehoboth Methodist Episcopal Church began holding meetings in 1827. In 1853, the first meetings of the Seventh United Presbyterian Church began and in 1860 the Frankford Avenue Methodist Episcopal Church formed. The first Roman Catholic church in Northeast Philadelphia began in 1843 and is still known today as St. Joachim's Roman Catholic Church. Fifteen other churches of various denominations would be established in Frankford through 1928.

In 1854, Frankford found itself a part of the city of Philadelphia due to the Act of Consolidation. A village that once had a great sense of community and a deep, rich heritage and history began to find that identity disappearing as it became just another section of Philadelphia. In 1905, the Historical Society of Frankford was organized to preserve the town's history so that it could be told to the generations that would follow in the 20th century. The final piece that would connect Frankford with the rest of the city and would also mold Frankford Avenue into the business district that we know now today is the Market–Frankford Elevated (the El). Today Frankford is seen as one of the next sections of Philadelphia to go through resurgence. With easy access to center-city Philadelphia via the El and the vast number of businesses along Frankford Avenue, many are discovering Frankford again as a great place to reside.

One

STREET SCENES

The Jolly Post Inn and Tavern is one of the oldest and most historic buildings in the area. It was located on the west side of Frankford Avenue, just north of Orthodox Street. Dating back to 1682, the Jolly Post was the center of town, where people from Philadelphia would enjoy a summer afternoon, and local men would gather to discuss the Revolutionary War and the Civil War. This spot today is the American Pants Company.

This station once stood on the west side of Frankford Avenue, just north of Unity Street. Built in 1894, many churches would make use of this to ride up to Chalfont, Pennsylvania, for picnics.

This house at 4276 Orchard Street in Frankford looks like any other early-American home, but what makes it unique is that it was the first mortgaged home in America. On April 11, 1831, Comly Rich, the local lamplighter, borrowed $375 from the first building and loan in America.

The first building and loan in America was formed here at the Park Hotel. Constructed in 1760, the building was located on the east side of Frankford Avenue at the north end of Womrath Park.

Once located at Frankford and Oxford Avenues, the Seven Stars Hotel was built early in the 19th century. It was a stopping place for Bucks County farmers as they brought their goods down to Philadelphia. The hotel was later owned by John O'Brien of the O'Brien Circus.

This tollhouse stood on Oxford Avenue near what is now Oxford Circle along Route 1, Roosevelt Boulevard. This peaceful scene is a far cry from the busy intersection that it is today.

MAIN ST. N. OF SELLERS ST. FRANKFORD PA.

Here is a view of Frankford Avenue looking north above Sellers Street. Frankford Avenue, "The Ave," still stands today as the center of business for Frankford and the surrounding area.

Pictured here is the front entrance to Cedar Hill Cemetery, where many of Frankford's well-known residents and Civil War soldiers are buried. Some of the names seen here might be recognizable as street names, such as Horrocks and Wakeling.

This photograph, dated 1922, shows the dedication of the World War I monument at Memorial Stadium. The stadium is currently used by Frankford High School.

Once part of Large's Woods, Northwood Park has always served as a quick getaway from city life for Frankford residents. Notice the grandstand in the center and the fence surrounding the park.

Frankford is proud of the special place that the Marquis de Lafayette held in his heart for the people of the town. Frankford celebrated his visit and was proud of the hometown veterans whom Lafayette honored, such as Gen. Isaac Worrell.

This photograph displays the typical merchant that conducted business along the avenue. Most merchants or business owners would have the first floor of their house dedicated to their business and then reside on the remaining floors.

Many mills and factories made use of Frankford Creek for centuries. Notice the arched bridge over a much wider creek than what is there today.

A usage that would be unheard of today, this garden runs all the way down to the bank of the Frankford Creek.

One of the Clark and Hunter teams is seen here. The colonial house to the right was last used as a residence by Dr. Richard Allen. Formerly it had been the residence of the Gillingham family.

This photograph was taken in front of the North Baptist Church, which was erected in 1897. Judging by the size of the horse, these people probably did not have any problems driving through the snow.

This photograph shows Keegan's Hotel, which stood on the west side of Frankford Avenue. Today this is the site of the Bridge and Pratt Septa station.

A group of school children are seen outside of a market building on Paul and Ruan Streets. It is not certain whether the roof is going up or coming down, but this market building was, at the time, one of the oldest in Frankford.

This store and shop with the double windows were very ancient, probably dating to the Revolutionary War period. In 1840, the shop was a grocery store kept by a Mr. Blomley. John Cooper became his clerk and eventually bought the business and moved into the store to the left. He then opened a china store in the building. In the doorway are John and his wife, Sarah (Robert Burn's daughter). The young man with the broom and apron is Cooper's grocery clerk, Joe Shafer. This picture was just taken before the demolition of the structures about 1876.

Pictured here is the Knights of Pythias Greenwood Cemetery located on Asylum Pike, which is now known as Adams Avenue. The land was chartered on October 26, 1869, as the Greenwood Cemetery Company of Philadelphia.

Here is a photograph of Frankford Avenue just south of Arrott Street decorated for the Theodore Roosevelt and H. W. Johnson campaign.

A great blizzard struck Frankford on March 12, 1888. The streets of Frankford were blocked for

three days before clearing began.

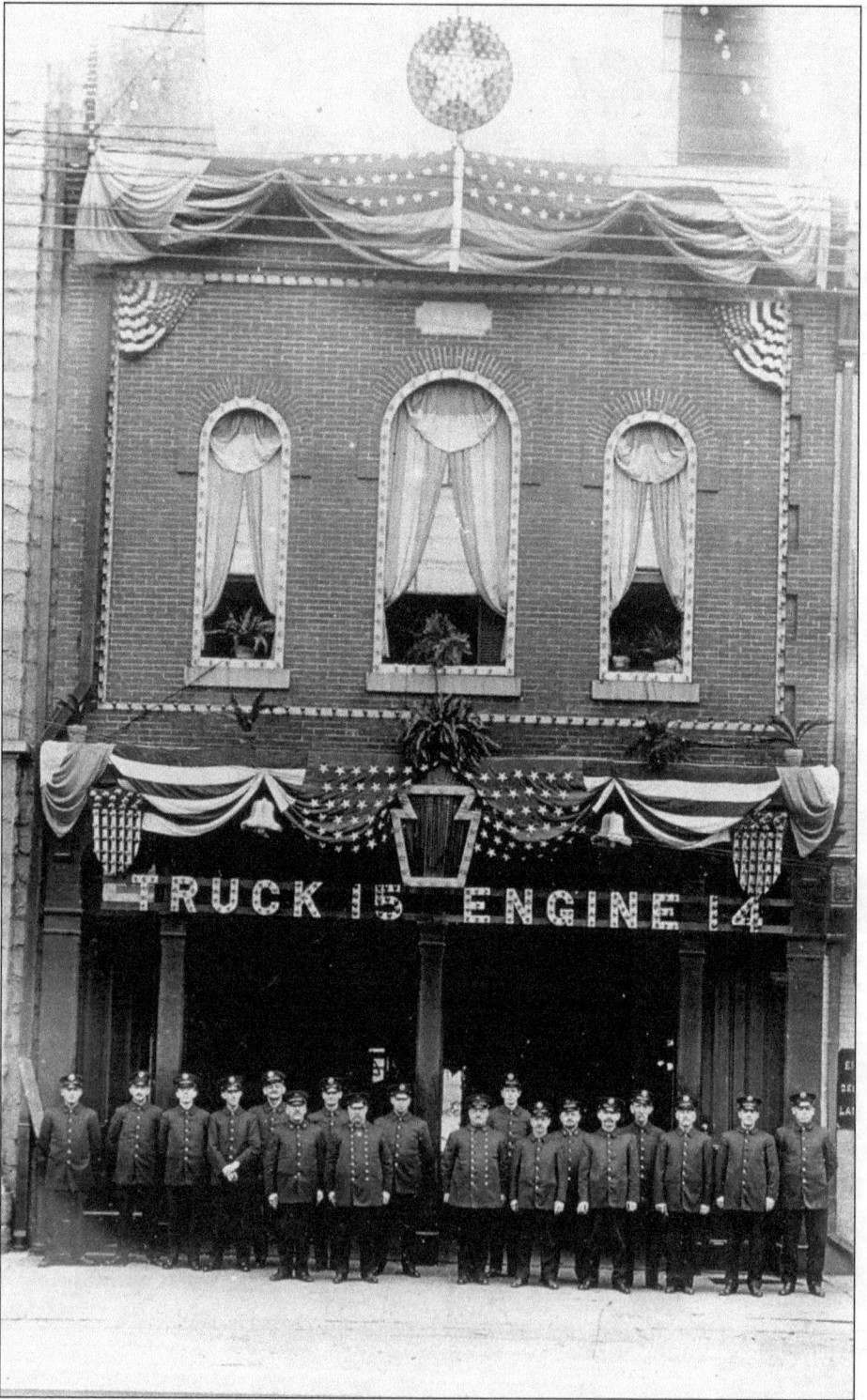

Engine 14 is seen during Old Home Week in 1909. Instituted in 1793, the organization's first firehouse was built in 1847 and then rebuilt in 1881.

This photograph shows Engine 7, which was also decorated for Old Home Week in 1909.

Old Ironsides was Frankford's first fire engine.

This was another one of Frankford's fire engines, named Old Decatur.

The Rescue Hook and Ladder Company was established in 1853 at Paul and Tacony Streets. Aaron Y. Coats Flour and Feed Store is seen in the background.

The Union Bucket Company on Franklin Street was organized in 1816. The building has since been torn down.

This tent was set up at Frankford Avenue and Oxford Pike to sign up recruits of State Fencibles in April 1917.

N.o7 FIRE Co's NEW HOME and GAS OFFICE FRANKFORD PA.

PHOTO BY WM. SLIKER BRIDESBUR

Frankford's police station, later an insurance office and Number 7 Fire House, is seen here on the left.

Two

CHURCHES

The First Presbyterian Church
was originally built in 1770. The
present church, seen here, was
erected in 1859.

The first Friends meetinghouse was located at Waln and Unity Streets.

The second and current Friends meetinghouse is located on Orthodox Street at Penn Street.

Pictured here in 1912 is St. Joachim's, which is northeast Philadelphia's first Roman Catholic Church. Located on Church Street at Griscom Street, the parish was officially founded in 1845 and still continues to serve Frankford today.

Pictured here is the Frankford Avenue Baptist Church in 1909.

Trinity African Methodist Episcopal Zion Chapel was erected on March 6, 1877.

The Second Baptist Church of Frankford is located on the northeast corner of Meadow and Mulberry Streets. First erected in 1883, it was rebuilt in 1905.

Pictured here is the side view of Central Methodist Episcopal Church as it appeared along Franklin Street, which is now Griscom Street, and Orthodox Street. Notice the lack of a paved street and the fencing around the church.

The second oldest African Methodist Episcopal church in the country, Campbell African Methodist Episcopal had grown from Bethel Church in Philadelphia. The first church building was built about 1836.

Rehoboth Methodist Church is located on the east side of Paul Street. The church was remodeled in 1879, and the parsonage was built in 1889.

Originally located on the west side of Leiper Street, and adjoining the old stone quarry, the first Presbyterian church was developed on this site and then moved to Tackawanna Street. This building was demolished in 1928 after serving many years as residences.

Pictured here is the Seventh United Presbyterian Church located at Orthodox and Leiper Streets.

This crowd gathered at St. Mark's for the laying of the cornerstone of the parish house.

Three

FRANKFORD HOSPITAL

The original Frankford Hospital building is pictured here in 1907. It was the former home of Thomas and John Willraham.

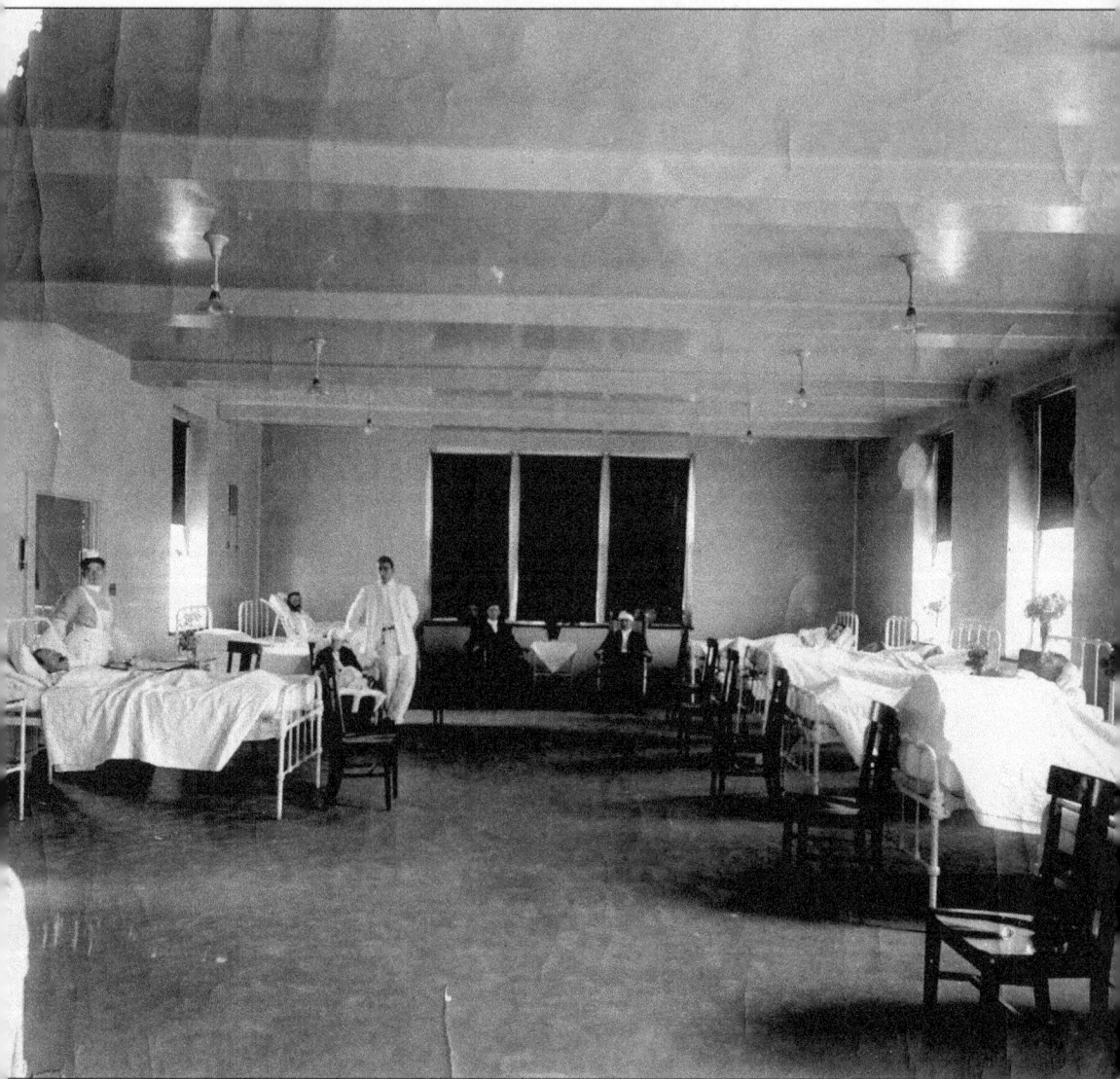

This view shows patients and staff inside the hospital.

This early photograph shows one of Frankford Hospital's first staffs of doctors. Dr. Thomas Proce can be seen sitting on the left and Dr. Louise English is seated in the center.

Back in the early days of the Frankford Hospital, the nursing staff built the reputation that the hospital has today.

This is a glimpse at what your surgery room would look like in case you had to be patched up from some small mishap.

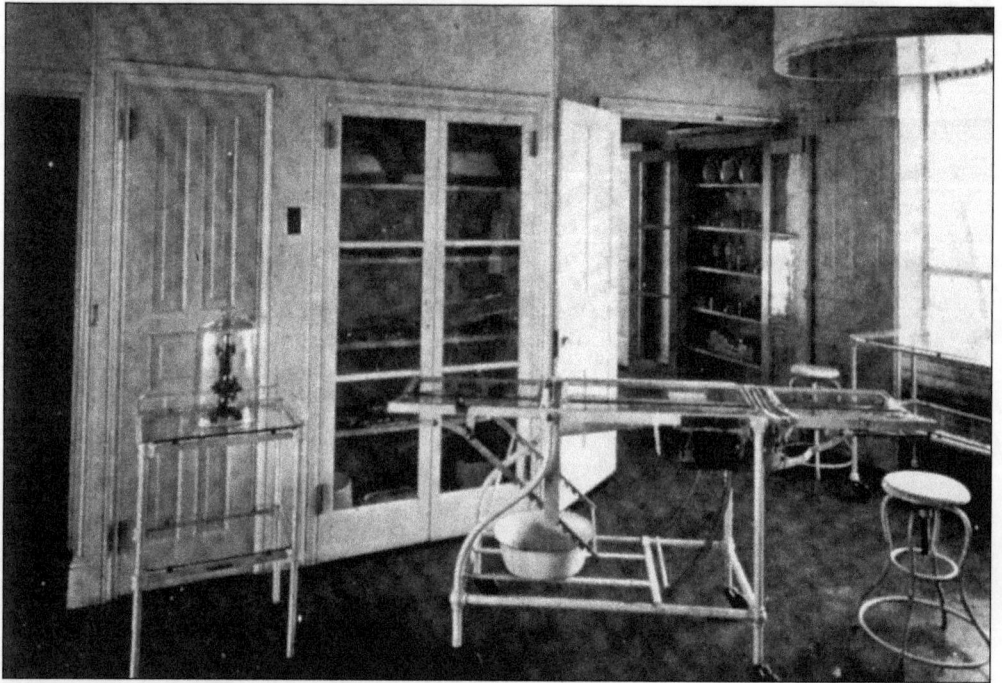

This image shows what the surgery room looked like around the 1920s, with almost a decade of medical and technological advances.

Opened in 1910 in a row house at 4930 Frankford Avenue, a total of 340 infants were born here. The ward was named after Adele Schlichter, who was very active in opening this ward. She was also later named as the first woman to the board of directors.

From the earliest days of the hospital, the women of the Auxiliary have raised money to provide new equipment and care for the poor. For many years, the June Fete was a popular fund-raising event. This picture is from the 1954 June Fete.

This photograph shows the staff preparing meals in the early days of the hospital.

This staff member is cleaning up after meals.

Four

SCHOOLS

Frankford's first schoolhouse was erected in 1821, and Isaac Shallcross was the first schoolteacher.

This photograph shows the Frankford Friends Schoolhouse during class time. The teachers pictured are Caroline W. Smedley, at the desk, and Alice Smedley, in the doorway. The children are, from left to right, the following: (first desk row) Eleanor Haslan; (second row) Howard Hills, Amanda

H. Chase, and three unidentified children; (third row) Isaac Schliditer, Ethel Haslan, Margaret M. Hilles, Alexander Henry, Lattie Wilkinson, and Howard Burtt; (fourth row) Walter Markel, Elizabeth W. Hilles, Walter Heston, Anna T. Harding, Emily Wolstenholme, and Isabella Oldham.

The Friends schoolhouse, located on the corner of Orthodox and Penn Streets, was erected in 1868 and is still used today.

The first Marshall School was erected in 1840.

The Wm. W. Axe School was constructed in 1904.

The Whitehall School was built in 1858.

Alexander Henry School, located at Paul and Unity Streets, was built in 1890.

The James Seddon School was opened in 1897 in the old Swedenborgian church on Hedge Street.

The first public kindergarten was opened in 1897 in the old Dr. Pickering house. This house is the current Grand Army of the Republic Museum.

The Decatur Primary School was opened in a rented building on Orchard Street in 1864.

The Wilmot School for African American children was rebuilt in 1874. The original school was built in 1840.

The current John Marshall School, which is still in use by the Philadelphia School District, was built in 1909.

Shown here during Old Home Week in 1909 is the Frankford Public Library. Before the age of computers, what school project would ever be finished without a trip to the library?

Built in 1769, the Waln Street School master house stood on the north side of Cloud Street and the west side of Waln Street.

The first Frankford High School was built at Oxford Pike and Wakeling Street. Behind the school in the background is the old Wistar barn.

This picture shows the Frankford High School as it appeared in 1912.

George Alvin Snook was the founder, teacher, and first principal of Frankford High School.

This photograph of Frankford High School is from the 1918 yearbook. Not much has changed since this picture was taken. From its beginnings in 1910 as an annex of Central High School, Frankford High School has served the neighborhood and made it proud as one of the best-known schools in the Philadelphia area.

Five

FRANKFORD EL AND SEPTA

Stationed at Arrott Street and Frankford Avenue are the 59, the 75 and the K route buses.

Looking closely at this photograph of the building of the Elevated through Frankford, you will notice what makes this neighborhood just a bit different. For the construction of the El to be approved, local businesses demanded that the beams for the structure be built in the middle of Frankford Avenue, allowing customers to walk unobstructed down the sidewalks.

Seen on the new tracks of the Market–Frankford line, this early elevated car is primed and ready to run.

It is easy to see from this photograph how much the El took away from the wideness of Frankford Avenue.

Shown here is the corner of Frankford Avenue and Bridge Street as it appeared before the completion of the El.

This is a photograph of the last bit of work at the end of the line at the Bridge and Pratt station, now known as the Frankford Terminal.

Mayor Joseph Hampton Moore of Philadelphia is seen here dedicating the new elevated system and Frankford Terminal in November 1922.

Here is a view of the crowd that turned out for the dedication of Frankford Terminal in November 1922.

People did more than just show up for the dedication at the terminal, as you can see by the family in this photograph.

One of the events held during the day of the dedication was a historical parade down Frankford Avenue underneath the newly completed El.

The Philadelphia Rapid Transit station at Bridge and Pratt is shown here. The station eventually gave way to what is known today as the Frankford Terminal, or simply Bridge and Pratt.

The Route 3 trolly is seen under the El.

Pictured here is the Route 58 trolley. Notice that it is headed in the direction of Wissinoming.

The Route 58 bus makes its way up Orthodox Street, coming up to the intersection at Oakland Street.

Six

HOUSES

The Womrath Summer House is legendary in Frankford. Located at Frankford and Kensington Avenues, where Womrath Park is now located, it is said that even Thomas Jefferson had visited the summer house and read the Declaration of Independence publicly for one of the very first times.

Chalkley Hall is known not only worldwide but also in the literary world, thanks to the poem "Snow Bound" by John Greenleaf Whittier. The western part of the house was built in 1723 by Thomas Chalkley, who at the early part of the eighteenth century was one of the world's

best-known travelers and ministers. The hall itself was built by his son-in-law, Abel James, between 1741 and 1789. Torn down in the 1930s, Chalkley Hall is now stored at the State Museum of Pennsylvania. Some of the contents and statues are kept at the Historical Society of Frankford.

William Foulkrod, whose house is seen here, was a U.S. representative from Frankford between 1907 and 1910. He died in office in 1910 and is buried in Cedar Hill Cemetery.

Seen here is the residence of Herman Blum, John Walton, William H. Burns, and F. Hormann, which is still a private residence today. This was one of the great former summer homes located on Leiper Street.

This is the residence of Thomas Green on Leiper Street above Arrott Street.

Shown here is Eberly House, which was later occupied by a Mrs. Kane for many years. A Mr. Daree then resided here until his death. The house was then torn down to make way for the Forum Theater, which, in turn, no longer exists. This house was located on the east side of Frankford Avenue just below Bridge Street.

This home was originally located at the northeast corner of Frankford Avenue and Kinsey Street. Behind the house was Wakeling's Book Bindery Shop. The classic *The Last of the Mohicans* by James Fenimore Cooper was bound in this bookshop.

Located on Tacony Street, the Worrell House was built during the 18th century. The older parts of the farmhouse are located to the left. The property was later part of the Smedley Brothers Lumber Yard in the 1930s.

The house shown here was located at Tacony and Margaret Streets. Notice the age of industry that was beginning to come into the area across from the farmhouse. Frankford eventually lost all of its farms to factories.

Shown here is the intersection of Frankford Avenue and Unity Street. The Whitelock House was located on the east side of Frankford Avenue below Unity Street. This is one of the best shots of Frankford Avenue as a residential street.

Seen here is the residence of the Womrath family. Notice the row houses in the background that were starting to appear.

Summer Hill was located on Arrott Street and Castor Road. The home of the Large family, the house is pictured here in 1909.

The Horrocks house was located on Asylum Pike, which is now Adams Avenue.

The Overington residence was built by Fisher for William Overington in 1847 on the very site of and utilizing materials from a much older house. The older house belonged to the Smiths, who owned along this property, which is Leiper and Overington Streets to the present northwest corner of Pratt and Penn Streets.

Seen here is the home of Horrace Greenwood as it was in 1912. The house was built by Greenwood's father and stood at Leiper and Foulkrod Streets. It was demolished in 1926.

Taken in February 1912, this image looks west on Orthodox and Leiper Streets starting from the Jefferson Justice House to the M. Savage House.

Capt. Stephen Decatur's mansion, Millsdale, was located on Powder Mill Lane, which is now Adams Avenue at Castor Avenue. The farm was once owned by William Lane until Captain Decatur purchased the property upon his retirement from the sea.

Strawberry Hill was the home of the Welsh family and also stood on Powder Mill Lane. Members of the Welsh family are seen in this photograph.

The residence of the Rowland family, pictured here in 1909, was located in what was then known as Rowlandville.

This homestead stood on the west side of Frankford Avenue and south of Pratt Street. It is pictured here in 1909.

Seven

SPORTS

This is an early photograph of the football team from Frankford Athletic Association. In the 1890s, many neighborhoods and organizations began to have their own athletic associations, and many were very competitive. Frankford's would grow into something not only special but historic.

In 1905, the Frankford Athletic Association won the league championship for baseball.

Many Frankford High athletic standouts have made the community proud. Pictured here are some of the school's athletes in 1918. The athletes are, from left to right, Harry M. Volandt (track), Harry Barefoot (soccer, baseball), and Charles W. Dunnett (track).

FRANKFORD
Yellow Jackets

Official   Program

Published Weekly By The
FRANKFORD ATHLETIC ASSOCIATION
Member of The National Professional Football League.

Price Ten Cents

The legend that grew out of Frankford Athletic Association is the Frankford Yellow Jackets. The Yellow Jackets played first as a community team but soon grew into a professional organization that joined the NFL in 1924. Just two years later, the team won the NFL Championship. This is one of the game-day covers from 1926.

FIRST TIME IN PHILADELPHIA

BOBBY CALHOUN'S LOUD SPEAKER SAYS

PROFESSIONAL FOOT BALL

under Arc Lights

★ ★ ★

ALL AMERICAN STARS

Yellow Jackets

VS.

BROOKLYN

Friday Night, Oct. 2, 8.30 P. M.

Phila. Municipal Stadium

50,000 Seats at $1.00

Yellow Jacket Band in Attendance   FREE PARKING

The Yellow Jackets took part in another historic event when they hosted the NFL's first-ever night football game against Brooklyn at Municipal Stadium in Philadelphia. Notice that all of the seats were $1.

Yellow Jackets

GAMES

To be Broadcast

EVERY SATURDAY

over

STATION WFKD

(Play by Play Description)

Listen In!

WITH A

VICTOR - ZENITH
ATWATER KENT
R. C. A. RADIOLA
COLONIAL - MAJESTIC

ALWAYS THE FINEST in RADIO

NORTHEAST
RADIO CO.

4824 Frankford Avenue
Jefferson 1900

6300 Torresdale Avenue
Mayfair 2563

6027 Torresdale Avenue
Jefferson 4323

Many Yellow Jackets fans would spend their Saturdays next to the radio trying to listen in on the action. Here is an advertisement for the games hosted on WFKD.

80

NFL hall of famer Guy Chamberlin played for the Yellow Jackets between 1925 and 1926 and coached the 1926 championship team.

Herb Joesting is considered by some as the greatest player to put on a Yellow Jackets uniform. The greatest fullback in college history, he once racked up 179 yards in 21 minutes of play.

The pre-NFL years were just as competitive for the Yellow Jackets as the later years. Frankford wanted to field a quality team, and only the best would do.

In just two short years, Frankford was able to field world champions in the NFL. Newspapers from coast to coast would report on the Yellow Jackets, and business men from as far away as London would ask about the team when they visited the states.

Frankford's stadium stood at what is now Frankford and Devereaux Avenues. This is one of the rare photographs from inside the stadium. The photograph shows the north stands and reveals that not many seats were left empty on game day.

Even rarer are actual close-up game-day photographs. This is a look at the game played against the Detroit Panthers.

Another great rival for the Yellow Jackets were the Dayton Triangles. This is a photograph from

the 1926 championship season.

The 1931 season of the Frankford Yellow Jackets would be the last. Due to the Depression and the destruction of their home stadium, the Yellow Jackets folded. In 1933, the franchise rights were sold to Bert Bell, who founded the Philadelphia Eagles.

This aerial view shows the Yellow Jackets' stadium during game day.

A popular page on the weekly program of the Yellow Jackets was the Jackets' very own comic strip. This comic depicts the previous week's game against a team from Wildwood, New Jersey, in 1927.

Frankford Wins National League Football Cro

Yellowjackets Play Tie With Former Champions

Phillies Win Soccer From Fall Rive

Tex Rickard Gets Control of His Palace

Takes Match in Penn A. C. Indoor Play

The *Philadelphia Record* proclaims the Yellow Jackets as world champions of the NFL.

Eight

THE PEOPLE
OF FRANKFORD

This is an inside look at a Frankford family that was enjoying dinner. This note on this photograph reads "The Dining Room of the O'Neill Family." Like many families in Frankford, eating together and catching up on the day was an essential part of the typical day.

The people of Frankford were very patriotic and sent many of their children to war. This parade is celebrating Decoration Day and remembering those who gave their lives for this country. Decoration Day is now Memorial Day.

Each one of the girls pictured here in 1920 represents one of the original 13 states. This photograph was taken on the lawn of the Overington Estate, which is now Overington Park on Orthodox Street.

Dark Run Woods was a popular picnic location for the people around Frankford. This photograph shows the Robert Ashby family and friends at Dark Run in 1912. Dark Run ran along what is today Cheltenham Avenue.

Many organizations came together to build Community Field, which today is used by Frankford High School. Pictured here is the Father's Association during the ground breaking in 1922. The field is also known as War Memorial Stadium.

This is another photograph of a group in Dark Run about 1912. It is difficult to realize that many row homes now stand where these rolling hills and wildflowers once did.

Dr. Deacon moved to Frankford in 1849 and originally resided at the corner of Frankford Avenue and Unity Street. The rector of Trinity Church Oxford in 1859, he resided there until his death in 1886. Deacon was a tireless worker, and it is said he never had a vacation in eleven years.

Daughters of the American Revolution gather outside of the Waln Street Friends meetinghouse.

Seen here are possible future draft picks from the Frankford Yellow Jackets.

The Young Republican Club of Frankford poses for this photograph.

Children march in a parade at the southeast corner of Paul and Church Streets. They are possibly students from Mater Dolorosa Catholic School.

The dedication of the tablet memorializing the visit of the Marquis de Lafayette was erected in 1913. Pictured in the front row are, from left to right, Robert T. Corson, Thomas Crieghton, Guerusee A. Hallowell, and Dr. John Valler. The men standing near the tablet are unidentified.

Franklin Smedley was the second president of the Historical Society of Frankford, serving from 1908 until his death in 1924. He was known as a community man who devoted any time he had to Frankford, from the business association to laying the cornerstone of Frankford High School. Born in Frankford in 1849, he spent his entire life there.

Known as "Mr. Frankford," Howard Lee Barnes was responsible for keeping the historical society strong during the second half of the 20th century. Barnes wrote and published two books on Frankford, *A History of Frankford*, and *A Scrapbook of the Frankford Yellow Jackets*.

The board members of the historical society were photographed in December 1952 during the presentation of the booklet "A Historical Background of Frankford." The board members pictured here are, from left to right, as follows: (top row) Charles Schroder, Omar Shallcross, and Raymond Hilles; (bottom row) David Williams, Dr. Charles N. Sturtevant, Mabel Corson, Caroline Smedley, Edna Worrell, and Brewer Walton.

Nine

BUSINESSES

Starr's Café was located on the southeast corner of Frankford Avenue and Margaret Street. None of the names of these individuals are known, but most likely the owner is to the left, and, of course, one of Frankford's finest is on the right.

The Berkshire Mills stood at the corner of Church and Worth Streets.

Thomas Castor and Sons Carriage and Wagon Works, located on the northwest corner of Frankford Avenue and Overington Street, is seen here in 1909.

This photograph looks west up Foulkrod Street at Frankford Avenue. Shaw's drugstore can be seen on the left and Horitz Produce is located to the right.

The Bell Company is dominating in this photograph of the northeast corner of Sellers Street, looking from the east side of Frankford Avenue. A tea shop is to the left.

Looking west from Frankford Avenue up Unity Street, Wright's Institute is seen in the back. McMullin's grocery store, later McKinley's Tavern, is seen here on the right about 1922.

The Koehler florist shop was located on Frankford Avenue and Granite Street. Jean Koehler and his sons Raymond and Julius are pictured.

The Cedar Hill Hotel was located off of Frankford Avenue just above the present-day Cheltenham Avenue.

This photograph looks over the stone quarry located off of Adams Avenue toward Frogmoor Mill. In the background, from the left, are Ruan and Leiper Streets.

Looking east on Frankford Avenue from the northeast corner of Orthodox Street, the Thomas the Hatter shop is visible in the forefront.

This shot was taken on the east side of Frankford Avenue, just south of Church Street. The Union Market is on the south corner with Kilbride's Restaurant next to it. The Presbyterian Church is seen in the back.

Looking at the northeast corner of Frankford Avenue and Foulkrod Street, the McCalley Blacksmith shop and S. W. Smith's Saloon can be seen.

This view looks at the east side of Frankford Avenue, just south of Unity Street. Notice the two forms of transportation in front of this row of shops. It would not be long until cars and buses replaced the bicycle and horse and wagon.

The Second National Bank is decorated for Old Home Week in 1909.

The Frankford Trust Company was chartered on January 5, 1888.

Shown here is the west side of Frankford Avenue north of Unity Street. A cigar shop is to the left with H. Kurtzman Upholstering next door. The Frankford station of the Philadelphia–Reading railroad is next to the right, and St. Mark's is seen all the way to the right.

The Empire Theater was nestled in between shops on Frankford Avenue. The Empire was one of many theaters that stood in Frankford.

It would be great if prices like this still existed.

Numerous area homes are listed here.

Keystone Stores Co.

Highest Quality At Lowest Prices in Town

4456 FRANKFORD AVENUE

— Meats —

FOR FRIDAY ONLY
SHOULDERS
Baby Spring

Lamb lb 10c

Lowest Price In Years For This Quality

Rack Lamb Chops   lb. 10c

FELIN'S CITY DRESSED

PORK SHLDS.
lb. 15c

LOIN LAMB   LOIN VEAL

Chops lb. 25c

ARMOUR'S STAR SLICED

Bacon pkg. 18c

CLOVERBLOOM

BUTTER   lb. 25c

CROSS-CUT, BOLAR, TOP MUSCLE

Roasts lb. 25c

"All Meat — No Waste"

— Delicatessens —

FOR FRIDAY ONLY
OUR SPECIAL BLEND

COFFEE
lb. 15c

A Flavor Not Forgotten
Lowest Price Ever Sold
Limited Supply

Home Made
Creamed Potato Salad
German Potato Salad
Cole Slaw
Combination Salad   lb **15**c
Indian Relish
Pimento Relish

NEW DILL

PICKLES 3 for 10c

Complete Italian Spaghetti Dinner
ENOUGH FOR 4 PEOPLE

Spaghetti - Mushroom Sauce
Grated Cheese

pkg. 25c
REGULAR 45c VALUE

FRESH SLICED

Luncheon Meats
¼ lb. 7c
LARGE VARIETY

Imported
SWISS CHEESE
The Holey Kind   ½ lb **23**c
AIR DRIED BEEF
A New Flavor

A trip to the supermarket today is much more costly than years ago.

Ten

AN ENDING WALK THROUGH FRANKFORD'S PAST

The Wistar Barn is seen as it appeared in 1901 on the current site of Frankford High School. This image serves as a reminder that Frankford was once a town of farms and country estates.

This guard stands at the main gate of the Frankford Arsenal in 1909.

This snow may look like nothing compared to what brings things to a halt today, but in 1909, this snowfall brought Frankford Avenue to a standstill on Christmas Day.

This photograph of the Jolly Post shows the snowfall of the blizzard of 1899.

Here is another view of the blizzard of 1899. The note on this photograph identifies Dr. Drexler holding up the newspaper. A good snowfall is a great way to relieve stress, even for doctors.

This photograph shows Frankford Creek and the width that it once was. The mill in the background is located at Leiper Street and Adams Avenue.

This is how the intersection of Penn and Bridge Streets once looked. Though the scene looks rural in this 1909 view, city development was just 20 years away.

One of the oldest pictures shown in this book is this image of the Old Dummy Depot in 1872. The Dummy cars preceded the Septa buses and trolleys of today. The man in the top hat to the right is Albert Worrell.

Spending a Saturday afternoon at Womrath Park was one way for the men seated on the bench to catch up on news. Long before the El and stores engulfed Womrath Park, the area was just as open and airy as any in the city.

Centered in this photograph is the Frankford Trust Company, but what jumps out is the building to the far right. E. L. Moyer Photography took about half of the photographs seen in this book.

Before the site was used for Frankford High School, the business association of Frankford built a country club at the site of Harrison Street and Oxford Pike. The Frankford County Club sported a nine-hole course.

Situated between St. Joachim's Roman Catholic Church and the convent was the convent bell. Most likely used to call students to school, its rope extends all the way down to the sidewalk.

The John Shallcross House stands at 4657 Penn Street. In this photograph, Shallcross and his wife pose at the gate of their home.

Built in 1901, this building was used for the Frankford branch of the U.S. Post Office.

Shown here is Harpers House, located on Worth Street. It is easy to tell that this is Worth Street by the Storage House on the corner. Notice the older colonials situated in the middle of the block, as well as the simple phone number on the side of the Storage House.

Located on Frankford Avenue, just above Foulkrod Street, was Vine Cottage, home of Dr. Ross and once the residence of a Mr. Wallet and also Samuel Huckel.

The oldest photograph found for this book is this 1870 image taken of the south side of Frankford Avenue, just south of Unity Street. Notice that Frankford Avenue is primarily residential; it even has front yards.

Located today farther up in northeast Philadelphia, the 15th Police District once stood at Paul and Ruan Streets in Frankford. The station pictured here was built in 1883, while the original station was built in 1861.

This view of Leiper Street looks north to Overington Street off of Orthodox Street. Overington Park is to the left with the Overington residence as it once stood.

The Comegy Paul mansion once stood at Nicetown and Powder Mill Lanes. It was originally owned by William W. Waln.

This is land behind Friend's Hospital, where it is believed that—well before the European settlers came through—the Native Americans of the area, the Delaware, had lived.

If you were to be told that this is the current area of Bridge and Pratt Streets, would you believe it? Elbow Lane once served as the entrance to Dark Run. It was located not too far from the current-day intersection for Frankford Avenue and Pratt Street.

Pictured is 4678 Tackawanna Street. During the Civil War, many soldiers were camped around the surrounding fields, and it is said that this house was a favorite resort for cakes and conversations.

In this interesting, undated photograph, a crowd is seen along Frankford Avenue coming up to the Philadelphia Railroad station. Despite the bustle around him, the little boy seen has no interest whatsoever.

The author chose the last two images of the book to represent the hard workers and business leaders who built Frankford into what it is today. This picture shows two of many such people through the centuries. Holme Painting was located at 1613 Unity Street. Seen here are Thomas (right) and Charles Holme.

One of the most important attributes of Frankford is its sense of community. For hundreds of years, it has been the people of Frankford who have made it one of the most well-known and historic neighborhoods of Philadelphia. From churches to civic associations, theater groups to historical societies, Frankford is the people. Pictured here in front of the Seven Stars Hotel is the District 10 Boy Scouts of America around 1922.

ACKNOWLEDGMENTS

I would like to thank most of all the two women who pushed for me to complete this book when it seemed too time-consuming and it started to interfere with work and the daily things in life: my wife, Denise Harris, who gave up time for the things that we enjoy doing together when we find time away from our jobs, and my mother, Bernadette Harris, who relived those days of my being in school and called every other day asking, "Is that book done?"

I want to thank all of the volunteers and board members at the Historical Society of Frankford: Paul Andell, Megan Forrestal, John Klak, Harry and Jean Lamb, Kim Miller, Edwin S. Moore III, Diane Sadler, Gilbert Schobert, and now Janet Bernstein. And a special thanks to our president, Debbie Klak, who opened the doors of the society to this Frankford kid to help spread Frankford's history. Thanks also to John Fenton and Ghosts of the Gridiron for some of the Yellow Jacket photographs.

To all of my family and friends who supported me in completing this little project here that I thought would take just a few weeks. A new and deep respect has been found for all of those fellow local historians across the world who have completed or are currently working on an Arcadia book.

I would like to thank Erin and the rest of the staff of Arcadia Publishing for their patience and assistance in getting this book on Frankford printed.

Finally, I would like to dedicate this book to two women who had called Frankford their home before going on to their home with God: my aunt, Jacqueline Colucci, who, like my mother, would have had been calling every other day, and also my wife's grandmother, Millicent Minter, who was always asking me about the Yellow Jackets.

www.ingramcontent.com/pod-product-compliance
Lightning Source LLC
Chambersburg PA
CBHW050623110426
42813CB00007B/1697